The Book of Ruin

Also by Rigoberto González

Poetry

Unpeopled Eden
Our Lady of the Crossword
Black Blossoms
Other Fugitives and Other Strangers
So Often the Pitcher Goes to Water Until It Breaks

Essays

Pivotal Voices, Era of Transition: Toward a 21st Century Poetics
Red-Inked Retablos

Bilingual Children's Books

Antonio's Card
Soledad Sigh-Sighs

Novels

Mariposa U.
Mariposa Gown
The Mariposa Club
Crossing Vines

Memoir

What Drowns the Flowers in Your Mouth: A Memoir of Brotherhood
Autobiography of My Hungers
Butterfly Boy: Memories of a Chicano Mariposa

Short Story Collection

Men without Bliss

As Editor

Xicano Duende: A Select Anthology by Alurista
Camino del Sol: Fifteen Years of Latina and Latino Writing

The Book of Ruin

Rigoberto González

Four Way Books
Tribeca

Library of Congress Cataloging-in-Publication Data

Names: González, Rigoberto, author.
Title: The book of ruin / Rigoberto González.
Description: New York, NY : Four Way Books, 2019.
Identifiers: LCCN 2018028725 | ISBN 9781945588327 (pbk. : alk. paper)
Classification: LCC PS3557.O4695 A6 2019 | DDC 811/.54--dc23
LC record available at https://lccn.loc.gov/2018028725

This book is manufactured in the United States of America
and printed on acid-free paper.

Four Way Books is a not-for-profit literary press. We are grateful for the assistance
we receive from individual donors, public arts agencies, and private foundations.

This publication is made possible with public funds from the
National Endowment for the Arts

National
Endowment
for the Arts
arts.gov

ART WORKS.

and from the New York State Council on the Arts, a state agency.

NEW YORK
STATE OF
OPPORTUNITY.

Council on
the Arts

We are a proud member of the Community of Literary Magazines and Presses.

PROUD MEMBER

[c|mp]

In memory of Justin Chin

Contents

Book I: The Book of Lost Souls

Book II: The Book of Ruin

I

The Book of Lost Souls

A Brief History of Fathers Searching for Their Sons

1. Parable

There's a man who sits on the shore every morning,
staring at the sea. And the sea stares back, defiantly.
It won't release its secrets. *I'll give you an answer
if I take what you're offering me,* says the sea.

When the man begins to weep, the sea yawns
with indifference. Tears are abundant here. As are
sinking ships and broken hearts and moons that drop
like shards of shattered windows. Prayers crumble,

brittle against the Caribbean wind. *There's nothing
in your skies or on your land I haven't swallowed.
Or spat right back.* The man, defeated, rises, drags
his shadow—a shadow? Or a piece of cloth, a flag?

The sea keeps reaching for a closer look. The figure
blurs into the landscape and takes his story with him.
Waves crash against the rocks as if that sudden exit
hadn't left the ocean waters floundering in wonder.

What was that? The question turns to driftwood
and knocks against the mass of land, thereafter
unanswered because the man never came back.
And so the sea sifts through its rubble once again

and again and again and again and again in order to
complete this puzzle—narratives left unfinished toss
inside memory forever. That's why the sea comes
to the shore each morning looking for a man.

2. The Mexican Revolution

There once was a man who traveled by boat
to arrive on Montezuma's soil. Not explorer
or conqueror but a father who had carried his grief
from China. His son had made that trip to Big

Lusong a decade earlier but he disappeared among
the marigolds—the bursts of rage and rifle fire
in Torreón. But the man believed his son
was still alive and so began his search. Just

like the other man who followed the coast
from Chiapas to San Diego, looking for
his wide-eyed boy who had joined the revolution.
The Mexican war had come to an end but not

the stories of the men who left their
tiny villages for worlds much larger than
their fathers had informed them. But how
do itinerant sons meet their fates?

On that night the shopkeeper stayed up late
to watch the torches on the horizon coming
closer. So the rumors were true: the soldiers
were pillaging the dreams of the foreign-born.

No time to regret not heading north
to the mountain made of gold, where men
like him weren't welcomed anyhow. But now
this. Now hoof. Now bullet. Now final bow.

The youngest soldier in the cavalry felt
his face grow warmer as his target's shirt
grew redder as the cries of panic mixed with
the frenzied cries of victory. What misery

befell los chinos de Coahuila on that night
when their adoptive country chewed her
insides out. The headline's odor drifted to towns
along the border. When the Asian populations

shrunk, the Norteños joked that they had sunk
into that hole dug to China. The headline's shriek
then reached the shore of Mexico by way of the man
gone mad, who had swallowed the scream

of the man he had shot and so he was cursed
to repeat that sound until he threw himself
into the sea. *I kept his suffering soul but I pushed*
his body back to the deserted beach. I didn't want

that much sadness inside of me, said the sea.
And that was the end of that until two other
men came to ask the great ocean, great witness
of triumphs and tragedies, if it had come

upon their sons. Question spoken one hundred times
before. Question to be spoken one hundred times
more. But this was an occasion the sea had never
seen: the father of a son who had killed a man

crossing paths with the slain man's father.
How they comforted each other knowing
they were not alone on their journey.
How they accepted consolation not knowing

about the terrible connection between
their sons. And that's why the sea kept quiet.
For even gods capable of fury can temper
their waters for a temporary act of mercy.

But silence too has outcome: blindness. The fathers
exchanged nods and moved on—one heading
north, the other heading east, both energized
by the encounter with another man

who loved his son so fully he couldn't
lose him to uncertainty. Call it folly, it's
the history of migration: life granting men
such cravings for adventure, curiosity, purpose

and ambition, their stories pass each other by
without notice, or collide—a strike that's
fatal, or inexplicably polite. What decides
if the outcome is heartache or glory?

Don't look at me, says the sea. *I too shift up
and down, back and forth. Even I don't know
where I'm going, how the journey will be. I'm
no less immigrant than you, no more the refugee.*

3. Tsunami

There's a man who sits on the shore every morning,
staring at the sea. He doesn't have any sons
left. They dispersed like a pool of fish when the sinker
strikes the surface of the water. The eldest took

the family boat, the middle son the net, the youngest
claimed the rods, the lines, and hooks, stripping
their father of his fisherman's estate though
he wasn't dead yet. His burden was a stroke

that left him trapped inside a body—a tackle box
that lost its key. A mermaid chewed on the tips
of her hair like seaweed before crawling up
the sand just to fling a mussel shell against

his skull. He didn't move. But inside he felt elated
that for once an object came towards him
instead of floating away like everything his wife
had brought him: kisses, kitchens, sons, the scent

of jasmine on her hands and feet. She dragged
into the tide their home—no, the entire street,
the village—uprooting lampposts and eucalyptus
trees now obscene with earthworms, their moistness

desperate at the separation from the soil.
His fingers had twitched just so as he reached
for his beloved who sank into the sea, the landscape
the train of a gown that swirled down after her.

Everybody drowned, oh figurehead of tragedy,
oh ravenous water god that snatches the air out
of every lung. After centuries of villagers taking
from your belly, you had to claim it all back—

each hard-won catch, each gasp from a child
whose first fish changes color in the bucket,
each bone stuck in the throat and every story
that followed. But your wrath hungered for

more than that: each blessing over the soup,
each time a man touched his bride beneath
the table during prayer, each time a man caressed
another man in the dark, every blush born of such

affection, and every encounter with pleasure
that ended with a mouth savoring its secret
into daylight. *Give it to me*, said the sea, *every
glimpse of your woman's nipple as she fed*

*each of your sons, every bristle of your lover's
beard found on the pillow and which you fondled
while the dawn peeked through the blinds. Every
ray of light. Every time you heard the coffee*

boiling on the stove and thought, What a lucky
man am I. I have everything. I have it all.
*No, you arrogant fool, I have it all—your
yesterday, the days before and the days ahead.*

*I swallow every minute you sit there begging
to get something back. I pick my teeth with
your disappointment. Some might think it
cruel that I let you live, you the one without*

*a voice, but what use is a voice when no one
heeds the warnings. Your kind gave me such
taste for waste that it became addiction,
and like any dog or snake I gave in to my rage*

when you weren't paying attention, when you
stood above me like a master and gazed
at the horizon as if you owned as far as
your eyes could reach. And I barked and I

hissed and told you that I too could play
that game but you wouldn't listen. What?
Is that a tear I see? Is it plump with shame
or regret? I'll savor it just the same. You,

sunk into the ruins is the story. You,
unheard is your fate. And mine. Now you know
what it's like to be me. You can whisper, scream,
it's pointless—nobody gives a fucking shit.

4. 43

There's a man who stands on the crest
of the mountain, staring at the land. He beams
with gratitude: no better friend to Guerrero's clans.
His father was a lumberjack and chopped

the pine for boiler, spit and cooking stove, his uncles
worked the mines for lead and gold, and he
the most industrious of them all—or so he's told—
saved enough to buy a plot to farm the tastiest

yams the town had ever known. He tilled
the soil at the crack of dawn and prayed for rain.
He combed the loam, kissed the sprout, wept
into the earth and the waters poured down,

swelling the meat, each tuber so plump the villagers
joked that it's what caused the ground to shake.
But quakes don't bring men to their knees
like reaping ñame, the clawing of hands keeping

rhythm to the harvest's wayward tune: *Oh
delectable mole with your weighty rump, how you
itch for caress when you twitch your nose
in the air, you flirt, no less striking in a dress*

made of dirt, you muscular calf in pantyhose.
The farmer laughs, but only in memory,
and he hikes each morning up the mountain
to recall it and every other sound the hills invoke:

his father's grunt each time the ax struck wood,
the whistle in his breathing as he nestled logs
into a load, the groan of hoisting it upon his back
and, hunched down, the steady footfalls headed

to the donkey cart. How the uncles pleaded
with his father, *Join the mines! Join your brothers
in the dig and give your son a more rewarding
task than gathering sticks for heaven's sake, all*

*alone with nothing but that little cross-eyed beast
to tease with riddles!* But his father carried on,
cutting firewood until his death. When the farmer
came to mourn him on the mountain Mountain said:

No grief, my friend, your father made no sounds
with sadness. And when you feel the urge to weep
come visit me and I'll remind you of what a joyous
man he used to be. I am the mountain that I am

because your father lived contentedly, and I
in turn have helped you thrive through hunger,
live with pain. We have survived together. If you
agree to treat me with respect I'll keep

you happy. Bring your son to me and I'll do
the same with him: he'll fill my days with sound
during his hours of labor, I'll fill his days with song
long after you are gone. The harvest after that

the farmer brought his son along. The boy
was quick to graduate from toys to tools
and had a knack for pulling out the yams
intact without a scar or scratch. And when

he giggled at his father trying to lift the treasure
sack his father felt the earth absorb the pleasure
of paternal exultation. And suddenly he understood
why the mountain never caved: each piece

of vegetable or mineral pulled out, each log
removed, was replaced with an expression of elation,
a gesture of goodwill. The legacy of reciprocity
continued until the son became an adolescent:

like his father and his father's father he had
interests independent of the men around him.
He left the farm and, with his father's blessing,
went to school. That too is the way of the land,

said the elders who nodded with approval
as the child picked up his books and pencils
and bicycled a path from the muddy rural road
to the city streets. They watched his intellect grow.

And so too grew his awareness of unfairness,
of the need to teach the people and prepare
to battle political corruption by rattling
Mexico's government with voice and education—

† † † † † † † † † †
† † † † † † † † † †
† † † † † † † † † † †
† † † † † † † † † † †

Oh proud papa, how you poured your hope
into the yams until they mirrored the disgraceful
fate of your beloved son after he and the other
42 were disappeared. Now you have to watch

this cemetery of a farm unburied limb
by limb and none of them his bones. Now
there's not a sound like happiness to spit
out of your mouth to offer to the mountain.

Both of you go numb. You've become
the man on the crest of the land of the dead—
earth force-fed the evidence of man's insidious
acts that rot its viscera away. Everyday you seek

his grave but Mountain doesn't speak. If it
exhales with the poisons in its lungs it surely
crumbles. Thus it remains inert, impervious
to your prayers—a cloud of seed flung over

the valley suspended in midflight. The brittle
Eucharist of hope not swallowed dissolves to
nothing on dry tongue. But don't give up, good
sir, even when passersby shake their heads

and say, *That's the madman who shrills as he punches holes into the mountain. His son is buried somewhere on this land so he digs anywhere he can. He hasn't found him yet. He never will.*

5. Portrait of a Father After His Son's Memorial Service

There's a man who sits on a bench
waiting for a train, though the trains
arrive and depart and the man remains
seated, the heaviness of resignation on

his face. As evening falls the light flickers
awake in the waiting room and a moth
begins to flutter in and out of sight
until it rests finally on the white bulb

above his head. All things come to calm
this way—even the trains. The cycles
of grinding metal stretch out into yawns—
each iron wheel a flower folding its petals in.

Night concludes its hymn. The man rises but
hesitates to leave this station of his cross.

The Incredible Story of Las Poquianchis of Guanajuato

1. Las Ánimas I

María Delfina, María de Jesús, María Luisa

We are three
unlucky stars. We are
unlucky three, the wardens who
traded their bodies for cells, their souls
for the honor to be the brothels' unholy trinity.

Men will judge
as easily as they will
love. And History, so male in his
cruelty, will write his fiction down in blood.
The true travesty is that his words are louder

than ours.
Don't be fooled.
Listen carefully. Embedded
in the falsehoods is our story. No, we are
not innocents. We certainly are the monsters

men created.
If we're to blame
for something, it's for making
men first, and then quenching their thirst
for the feminine limbs that taught them such affections.

What misery
cycle, what wheel
of misfortune that shrieks
when it spins, unspooling the thread
of our carnal sins. Oh fathers, oh sons, what a hell

we were in.
But don't pity us.
For the stray's death is not
so much punishment as it is salvation.
And dead we don't haunt your beds or your dreams—

we only are,
were, have been.
That you remember us
says more about your deeds than ours.
Forget us and we'll continue to be three

names once
anchored to evil
so vast it took three of us
to write the headlines. "Hellish"? Ha!
They called us the Gorgons, the ugly sisters

that turned
flesh into stone.
We beg not to disagree.
We put the fear of God in your small
human hearts, that's true. It's what mirrors do.

2. The Gospel According to María Luisa

Unbury the bodies, sisters, unbury
the wicked fruit of the wicked,
the wicked not us, not the greed
of women but the lust of men,
forever and ever, amén.

Forever and ever, these men, their
simple urges, their idleness. How they
spread their legs, how their small
hairy kings rule any house with
a door that welcomes them.

When I open the door to greet them
I'm taking sin off the streets—off
the streets, you heathens who deign
to stain the path to heaven's gate! Every
stone stays pure beneath our Catholic feet.

Will you vindicate me, Father, will you
tell the Lord what a good child I've been?
I speak through the Bible and anoint

the suffering of our fatherless girls, our
impoverished orphans, our Magdalenes.

On Sundays they wear veils
and pray the rosary, they kneel
not for man but God. I wipe
the taste of mortal off their tongues
with the back of a sacred cross.

Forever and ever the cross,
holy symbol of sacrifice and loss,
it's not the key to salvation—I'm
such a stupid woman—it's the lock.
I'm knocking, Jesus—knock knock—

I'm unbuttoning my blouse to give
you better access to my heart—
I'd give it you, Jesus. If you asked
for it I'd tear it out of me, my
unborn fetus, my unwound clock.

I'm the only virgin here, my Lord,
the rest have sinned against
their flesh. The Devil dragged

his vulgar tail into this harem
and tore away each maidenhead—

except for mine. I'm pure, I'm
yours if you will have this most
devoted of believers, touch me,
Jesus, lift this fever that devours
my inhibition during prayer hour.

I won't be tempted, I won't succumb
to the damnation of this house
of sin I'm slowly dying in but here
I stay to save these souls and earn
my place in His eternal grace.

Blessed be my righteousness,
blessed be my martyrdom,
blessed be the day I sit next to my
Lord, in service to my Master,
forever and ever, forever and ever, and ever and ever, amén.

3. El Tepocate's Tattoos

Delfina, his mother's name,
the "f" a rose, its head bowed
to dot the "i"; the "a" tadpole-
shaped, his namesake. It was

his mother's own design,
or rather her idea, to
replace the cursive letters
with images. Since she couldn't

read or write her son would
teach her, beseech her
to retrace the lines of ink
across his back. He lies

face down in bed. *Did
any of them die today?* she asks.
If *No*, her finger swims
up the urethra of the "l" then

trickles down the flower
stem. The tickle makes El
Tepocate shudder. *Mother,*
he will whisper. *Stroke*

that part again.
It's *Yes* today. She puts
her ear between his shoulder
blades to listen to his blood,

her breathing hot
and just as calm. She spreads
her palm over the cross
tattoo stretched across

his lower back and mutters,
It's for the best, isn't it,
mi rey? Decades now the men
have fled to labor for the gringo

and left the rest of us
unprotected and unfed.
The cost of glory in the next world
is a life of misery in this one.

May she rest in peace now
that she's shed her weary skin.
May God grant her wings.
María Delfina's lips travel

down El Tepocate's spine
and kiss the center of
the crucifix. His impotence
is innocence. She reaches

down his calf to feel his
third tattoo: she trusts this
tinted dagger that will not
give in to impulse—

like her father's had—
to harden in the drunken
dark to thrust.
And thrust.

4. Corrido de la Poquianchi Jesusa*

Señores, este es el corrido
de la Poquianchi Jesusa,
era mujer rete-trucha,
no importa lo que se haya dicho—
que le decían La Medusa
pero eso es puro ruido.

Ella nació entre los pobres
en el campo de Jalisco,
Madre quería puros hijos—
machos por trabajadores;
Padre se puso abusivo
pues Dios mandó cuatro errores.

Jesusa fugó de su pueblo
rumbo para Guanajuato,
pero en muy corto plazo
las otras tres la siguieron
pues ya tenía entre sus manos
hombre, negocio, y dinero.

Delfina juntaba pupilas,
Luisa la hacía de cajera,
Carmen cuidaba las mesas,
¡vean que exitosa cantina!
Jesusa era orgullo de jefa
con su casona de citas.

Llegaron los años sesenta
seguían las hermanas a engaños
a vírgenes secuestrando
sin que los padres supieran.
Les aseguraban trabajo
pero les daban condena.

El antro con más y más fama,
el pueblo tenía sus sospechas.
Jesusa decía que por viejas
les resentían tanta lana—
gente detras de las quejas
no ganan pan con la cama.

Problemas, querían evitarlas,
cerraron el bar en apuras,
se esconden con las prostitutas,

pronto fueron encontradas.
De rapto, extorción, y tortura,
Poquianchis quedaron culpadas.

Carmen ya había fallecido,
Luisa se dijo inocente,
A Delfina la cayó en la frente
una tina llena de ladrillo,
a Jesusa le tocó la suerte
de tener que cumplir su castigo.

Las revistas decían tantas cosas,
la tele prendía puro cuento,
más gusto le daba por dentro
a Jesusa que se vio famosa,
y así conquistó al carcelero,
la sacó y la hizo su esposa.

Y así concluye el corrido
de la Poquianchi Jesusa,
era mujer rete-trucha,
no importa lo que se haya dicho—
que le decían La Medusa,
¿verdad que no tiene sentido?

*On-the-spot translation: Gentlemen, this is the ballad of Jesusa la Poquianchi, who was a very smart woman, no matter what you've heard. That they called her Medusa is nothing more than noise. She was born among the poor in the rural state of Jalisco. Her mother had wanted sons, men to be hard workers; her father became abusive after God sent them four mistakes. Jesusa fled the town towards the state of Guanajuato but in a very short time her sisters followed, once she had in her hands a man, a business, and money. Delfina recruited the whores, Luisa was the cashier, Carmen took care of the tables, they built a successful cantina! Jesusa was the proud owner of a very popular brothel. The 1960s arrived and the women kept using deceit to kidnap virgins without their parents finding out. They promised them jobs and then sentenced them to a life in prison. The bar became more and more well known, but the town had its suspicions. Jesusa claimed that because they were women, people resented their earnings. Those behind the complaints didn't know how to make money in bed. They wanted to avoid any problems, so they rushed to shut down the bar. They hid with the prostitutes but were quickly found out. Las Poquianchis were accused of kidnapping, blackmail, and torture. Carmen had died by now, Luisa was found not guilty, Delfina met her end crushed beneath a bucket of bricks. Only Jesusa had the bad luck of serving out her sentence. Magazines made many false claims, the TV spun its tales, but it gave her a thrill since Jesusa became more famous. And that's how she courted the jailer, who took her home and made her his wife. This concludes the ballad of Jesusa la Poquianchi, who was a very smart woman, no matter what you've heard. They called her Medusa but it doesn't make sense, does it?

5. The Fourth Sister's Daughter

My mother was the oldest of the sisters
though by the time the crimes in the brothels
came to light she had already died.

This was her saving grace—why her name
vanished from public memory. I say
her name now—María del Carmen—

because I loved her, despite everything.
She too is part of the story, no matter how
much it pains me to admit it to you.

In many ways, she was the mastermind:
it was she who went to Guanajuato first,
not tía Jesusa. It was she who established

the first bar, not tía Delfina, and it was she
who kept the books, not tía Luisa. I know
because Abuela Berna told me my mother's

sins as punishment after she left me.
My heart aches when I tell you that it was
my mother who said, *Let's collect the poor,*

the unwanted, and turn them into whores.
Abuela Berna's threat was that this too
would be my fate if I didn't behave.

Abuela was afraid I had my mother's
wild streak, and for many years I wished
I did—it might have saved me from God.

But prisons were my destiny. I was
conceived in jail after Abuelo Isidro locked
my mother up to preserve her purity.

My father was the warden. Abuelo
took us in but only if my mother promised
to disappear into the night without

notice. He got his wish—one daughter
at a time until all four were gone and I
became his crutch as he shrunk

into the angry little man he always was.
Abuela fed him now and then.
My soul aches as I confess to cruelty

as well: the night he fell, I should have
helped immediately. I stayed in bed,
knowing he would bleed to death.

Only God can fine, but the Devil
asks for payment. And Abuelo got
what he deserved. As did my aunts,

I heard: tía Delfina met her end beneath
a bucket of cement; tía Jesusa will
likely rot in prison; and tía Luisa

is here with me, in the psychiatric
center run by nuns. Abuela brought me
to the convent before puberty

and here I am, cleaning vomit, shit,
and blood for all eternity. I pray
for the souls of the girls my mother

and her sisters murdered. I offer
my suffering as penance for what
my mother didn't pay. But I also answer

to the Devil: I sneak into tía Luisa's
room each evening and whisper curses
in her ear like Abuela Berna used to do.

The nurses are in awe at how,
by morning, my auntie chews away
her straps and claws a hole into the wall.

6. Death to María Delfina

An accident, the masons called it, but it wasn't.
María Delfina was murdered. I know this
to be fact. I know this to be truth. She was my cellmate.

María Delfina said she had the bad luck to be born poor.
The good fortune to be born a woman. A woman
had the power to survive anything. Including poverty.

The men up on the roof saw her coming. They knew
who she was. So they killed her. Not for sinning against God
or other women. But against men. She knew their weaknesses

for booze and flesh. She kept them in debt.
The only time she cried was when she talked about El Tepocate—
how she mourned his death. The same men who shut down

her businesses shot him. Her world ended there, not here
in this prison. I know this. On Sundays she walked to the chapel
to pray. The masons worked on the roof, mixing cement.

When the younger prisoners walked by they grabbed their cocks.
They spat on the older ones. María Delfina was the only woman
who wore a veil. *That's one of las Poquianchis*, I heard them say.

She knew mischief was planned. On her last morning alive she
gave me her Bible. On her way to the chapel the vat of cement
was dropped. The masons laughed. So did the wardens.

No other way could they bring María Delfina down. She was
La Mera-Mera, La Poquianchi—woman who fucked
the sex that would fuck us over. Stupid men. They didn't know

she was already dead inside. Hidden in her Bible was a picture
clipped from the newspaper. Her son's. She showed it to me
once. *My only regret was that he was born a man*, she said.

7. The Return of El Poquianchi

Ay, mujer, the things that went on in the back of that bar
even before the González sisters took it over. Truth was

those men fucked each other before las Poquianchis
turned it into a whorehouse. They weren't known as

las Poquianchis then. They were tía Jesusa and tía Delfina,
viejas from Jalisco who put up a sign that read *Guadalajara*

de Noche, but instead of stretching assholes the men
paid to stretch pussy. That's what Poquianchis means:

you leave very little forced open—wallets, mouths, legs.
It's all part of the game. Tía Jesusa asked my girls to stay

but they had bigger aspirations—D.F., L.A., Nueva
York, where the drag shows were catching fuego.

I retired my dazzling pair of heels and moved back
to my little ranch in Michoacán and remained untucked

for the rest of my life. I felt bad for those girls whose
babies died inside of them. Men are such wasteful bores:

they want the pleasure of firing their tiny guns
and will hide the bullet anywhere. In anyone.

Because I showed up in court wrapped in my favorite silk
rebozo I wasn't asked to testify. I would have spilled

every cold bean: how the police chief and the priest danced
in each other's arms then, how they were doing so again.

8. Las Ánimas II

We are the mummies
of Guanajuato you don't pay
to see. We are the bodies
of the daughters you sent away.

Yet here we are,
stubborn roots in the ground
you can't tear from
the heart of Mexico so easily.

We are your hidden
fantasies, your most forbidden
wants. Even now you
titter with anticipation

as you uncover us
to find our nakedness—
hipbone and buttock exposed.
Each fist a rose that withered

in our long wait in bed.

How male to make even this
about sex. It's what put us
here in the first place.

You dare disturb our sleep
and weep for us? Save
those tears for your unmarked
grave. Being found was worse

than getting lost.
We no more belong
to this world dead than we did
alive. Or will you prop us

up along the wall
with other mummies?
Charge admission?
Make your money?

No, of course not.
You claimed us and now
you will abandon us again.
We know the crooked

streets of your realm.
We too lost our way.
Who to blame: the hungry men,
the thirsty women, our

poverty, our bodies,
the cheap escape into the bar
with bottles and breasts?
Our families who released us

into polluted air? Oh fathers,
did you know what fate
awaited us? Oh mothers, did you
pray for safe return? Oh tiny

villages, you were the last
to let us go. We closed our eyes
as we bit into the soil for a final
taste on our tongues of home.

Hagiography of Brother Fire and Sister Smoke

1. Brother Fire

Feed me. Feeeed me. These are not
the only words it knows but they're
the only words it needs. And most times,
it's two words too many. Most times,

it's coaxed awake easily and on instinct
grinds the air between its teeth. Wild
creature, a stomach in a coat of quills that
chews through anything within its reach.

Was it the caveman who first discovered
its potential—weapon or tool? Was it
the caveman who first found out it could
possibly be tamed? The others saw a fireball

careening down the hill, the creature fastened
like a second skin. They heard a screech so singular
because this pain was new though it would be
an affliction another body suffered through

before the sun would set again. Oh sad
addiction to destruction, to the voyeuristic
impulse to stare at mass flower and wilt
into a shadow of itself. Oh dark ghost.

Prometheus was a fool to trust
the mortals who squander ingenuity
on ammunition. Even the man who
first held the wooden flute eventually

beat his neighbor with it, or so the story
goes. And when his instrument sang
out of tune he fed it to the creature who,
mad with insatiable hunger, ate the musician

too. The neighbor raised a bowl of water
to his lips and smiled as only the wicked
do. The gods looked over at the Titan
with his liver gouged and thought:

What pity to waste such a gift on
the petty, how tragic this magic turned
curse. When he figured out how to burn
things to the ground out of spite, revenge,

or the sheer perverse pleasure of causing
harm: that's when the human and this
monstrosity became inseparable. Thus
the history of fire became the history of man.

Man, imperious and arrogant, named it
to claim it, to deceive himself into
believing it was under his command.
Incinerator, he called it, Purifier, Blaze,

Consumer of Detritus and Waste. But
this creature answered to many other
names as well: Arson, Napalm, Immolation,
Fire Bomb, Dragon Breath, though in the end

its purpose was the same: to feed.
Feeed me, it begs, and its keeper complies
with cornfield, sugar cane, mesquite.
The more it eats, the more it craves,

mirroring its master's appetite so
greedy its hunger is mostly whim and
indulgence. *Feeeed me,* it whines, though
if the human ear could listen it would hear

Neeeed me. Need me, as in, *The want*
is all you, you belly aching baby, you
bored glutton, you bow-legged bitch
bastard son of a shit-slinging baboon.

That's right: you shove everything you
hate down my goddamn throat so how
else do you expect me to fucking talk,
you overstuffed bile sausage, you bloated

sac of bloody buffalo balls? The insult
darkens into carbon and drifts out of
earshot, just another disappearing act
for a thing that won't be. Selective erasure:

refusing to remember, aiming to forget.
And that's the reason, Fire, you've become
man's favorite pet. Prized in the cage of his
black stone heart you'll never die of neglect.

2. Sister Smoke

Call me Sister Smoke, groan that rises from
the burning wound, Brother Fire's fetid afterbirth,
its stink a sting—a thorn stuck in your throat—

the more you struggle to set it free the quicker
you choke. Once I come upon you it's best
to let it be. There is beauty in surrender—even

the blank-eyed fish embraces resignation in
the net and halts its flailing, locks itself into a stare
that beckons, Dare to love me just like this.

Don't let my reputation frighten you, I'm
more seduction if you will, I'm less the predator
the gossips make me out to be. My twin initiates

the kill and somehow I'm the villain. What
unbecoming accusation, what travesty.
If you really want to know my story, hear me

out instead of running from me. Come.
Get comfortable. Get closer.
Once upon a time

before I was a scavenger I was a messenger.
Before I was disgraceful I was the fateful
waving of plumes in the air, merciful signal

that warned all living things, *Beware the beast*
has left its lair. Not everyone escaped its path
but plenty did and word passed down

through generations that if by chance one
caught my dance on the horizon surely
there was danger there. Beware! It wasn't

quite affection but attention pleased me just
the same. My warnings were never called
heroic but I felt rewarded—instant recognition.

Before infamy you could say I was famous.
How I basked in my individuality. My body
seen apart from my brother's vile identity.

But fate can be so cruel, that's the rule.

The pride of presence comes with a price to pay.

Consider the royal forest that withers its leaves

when a wave of boorish rust weathers it—

a rotting graveyard ripe for Brother Fire's

ire. Consider the arrogant elk that locked horns

with a branch. I came upon this most idyllic scene,

which lasted seconds, until my brother cooked

the animal, then stripped the tree and picked

the carcass clean. Nature's beauty is ephemeral;

I'm a natural thing, as is my twin. Yet memory

clings to aftermath longer than it does

to the calm before upheaval. When man

domesticated Brother Fire to perpetrate his evil

I became guilty by association. I became

party to the rising temperatures, the droughts

and the pollutions. I lost my role as harbinger

with the industrial age and every iron cage

became my prison. A soaring spirit held captive
becomes reactive. If I asphyxiate and suffocate
you it's because I reciprocate the deed. See?

I'm simply an entity misunderstood. I only do
what you do to me. Since I'm no longer free,
the cloud of me becomes the shroud of you.

El Coyote and the Furies on the Day of the Dead

"where the Third World grates against the first and bleeds"
—Gloria Anzaldúa

The car overheats as you drive
through the Arizona desert at night.
You don't panic. You coast to the side
of the road. Above you, starlight
and not much else. The moon hides
behind the mountain, gets sliced
open when it tries to climb
over the crest. The spill is bright
and reaches the trees nearby.
Their shadows stretch like
the arms of those who died
of thirst here. You can't belie
this truth: you help them die—
the promises you make are lies,
coyote. They wait, you don't arrive.
The crooked lawyer paid your fine,
the sheriff shrugged. Justice denied
the dead who gather here tonight
to hound you, a curse goodbye
before they sink back into the dry
surface of the sand. You remain inside

the car but still hear the winds chime
out your crimes, coyote. The cries
of the wronged shatter glass, pry
you from your den. Your hackles rise
in distress as you realize
you grew paws, a tail. Your eyes
yellow and balloon with fright.
You're fucked. In your hasty flight
you leave a trail of warm scat behind.
A spectral steam fades into sky.

The Ghosts of Ludlow, 1914-2014

A century of silence is violence.

*

That winter a blizzard, a cold that crawled over
        the Sangre de Cristo Mountains and covered

                the foothills with a crust of ice.
                Everything whitened into bone.

        The clothesline snapped like a branch.
                A warning shot can be understood in

any language. The entrance to the coal mine dropped
        open like the mouth of a skull without eyeholes.

*

                Mining folk felt safest underground.
                        The pits were for protection from the chill

that had stretched into the spring. The pits
        were for protection from the wind that kept the walls

of each tent shivering all night.
　　The pits were for protection.

*

And somehow the kettle still sang,
　　its burst of steam a prized distraction

　　　　inside the deadness of the tent.
　　　　In the moment it was the thing

　　with most life. It filled the small space
　　　　with breath—an exhale so far away

from the hour it would take
　　the first bullet in its lung.

*

　　The horses crushed the quiet.
　　　　Their nostrils flared and suddenly

　　　　　　they looked quite human
　　　　　　　　in their rage. One foot sunk its hoof

into the face of a doll—an act
　　so cruel it had to have been deliberate.

The baby limbs stretched out in shock.
　　No mouth, no throat—no sound.

　　　　The horse shook its tail like a shrug.

*

Few things gathered the bodies
　　in the camp—a game of baseball,

　　　　a marriage, a christening, a strike.
　　　　And war, which darkened the light

in the tents, shadow upon shadow.
　　The soldiers first, then the smoke,

　　　　and then the fall of
　　　　a smothering sky.

　　The pits, so womb-like, a refuge
　　　　for the lambs while the wolf

devoured the tents, so sheep-like in their
            whiteness, so sheep-like in their bleating.

*

            The pits were for protection.

*

One evening the cook was making stew
            in the cauldron. A witch's brew, said

                        the children who dared themselves
                                    to come near enough to toss

                        a pebble of coal in the pot.
                                    The rocks bounced off the bellies

            of both cauldron and cook. The man cursed,
                        which only made the children giggle.

                        He chased them with the spoon.
                                    It made them laugh some more.

To teach a lesson, he grabbed a rabbit
　　　　by the ears. It kicked and splashed as he

submerged it under boiling water.
　　　　He trapped it with the lid.

　　　　　　The children screamed in terror,
　　　　　　　　imagining the bunny swimming

　　　through the scalding soup
　　　　　　only to reach scalding metal.

*

Grief for a dead child sounds the same
　　　in Greek or Italian or Spanish. Grief

　　　　　for eleven children has no language,
　　　　　　only numbness—

*

　　　　　　　　it hardens even the land.

Fires dissipated. Battles ended.
The miners rolled their stories up

and left the town of Ludlow, 100 years
empty except for an abandoned row

of shacks. Near the baseball diamond, a
memorial as neglected as the playing field.

A memorial rings hollow—it's for the solace
of the living. To reach the dead

walk toward the structures still standing,
their windows still looking in.

Listen closely for the ghost of a woman
tucking into bed the ghost of her son.

Lean in. That blank sound you hear?
The weight of the ghost of her kiss

as it passes through his head—
the collapse of absence into absence.

II

The Book of Ruin

Nothing beside remains. Round the decay
Of that colossal Wreck, boundless and bare
The lone and level sands stretch far away.

— "Ozymandias," Percy Bysshe Shelley

Apocalipsixtlán

1. New Beginning

There's a woman who squats on sand
    the color of midnight, we don't dare call it
ash. Instead, we marvel at how midnight
    comes and the woman appears to float
like a boat. Her white tunic a sail blowing
    with the hot winds from the north, where
it is rumored water still flows. We know
    about boats, we broke them down to bones—
a mercy killing. Since they wailed the loudest
    in the drought they had to be the first to go.

We tossed the priests into the fire pit next
    for filling us with false hope. And then
the politicians for telling us their lies. They
    told the truth finally but much too late to
change our minds about burning them alive.
    We tossed the teachers and the scholars
inside the barren wells, then dropped their
    wretched books on top of them and watched
the pages swell with piss and sweat. Steam
    hissed as they cooked beneath the bubbling

paper. We heard them boil and blister day
and night until their bodies softened into mush
and then hardened once again like plaster—
a pool turned frieze with jaws and fingers
jutting out. Those who held such wisdom
and refused to use it were the guiltiest of all,
and thus they earned the cruelest penance:
to drown in the pulp of what they prized
most—worthless words, incompetent ideas.
Despite our better judgment, we let the poet

live though with his mouth sewn shut. He
alone keeps the story of our insurrection. Each
night before we sleep we whisper in his ear
our precious secrets and stick a pin into his flesh
to keep them safe in case we die. If we awake we
repossess what's ours by pulling all the needles out.
His eyes dart left and right in panic during
visitations. We scurry down the dunes on fire
like a colony of scorpions. We are legion. We are
condemnation—promised land turned purgatory.

2. Mother

Tell us, Mother, should we journey to the north?
we ask the woman who squats on the sand.
She is old. So old we think of her as already dead.
During the purge we left her untouched even
after we had approved the suggestion to cut off
her fingers and toes to wear as talismans around
our necks. It wasn't pity that stopped us. We have
no compassion left. We had our rusty shears
sharp and eager. The old crone offered us
her crooked hands. Her eyes displayed no fear,

quite unlike the others who begged and cried
or opened up like sinkholes and ate the light
right out of their expressions. Weaklings bore us.
Let's save this one for another time, we said.
We might have forgotten she was still around
had the Muddies not arrived to try to steal her
from us. We fought them off with rocks—she's
ours. Anything this side of the crack in the earth
is ours. The crack is widening. What belongs
to us diminishes each season and that is why

we claim her as possession. *What do we name*
her? And the Smaller Ones among us, stupidly
sentimental, said we should call her Mother.

The rest of us scoffed. *Mothers are useless here!*
As are fathers and masters and kings. We argued
but they wouldn't budge. They reminded us
that all decisions are collective, argument's
divisive—we took the oath. So we agreed to it,
reluctantly, reasoning that Mother had no
meaning anymore. It was just an empty word

like all the others we have banished to the wells
with Those Who Came Before. We let Mother
wander aimlessly like a neglected pet until
we need a place to put our questions. The poet
hemorrhaged to death five nights ago and so
Mother will do until we come across the next
survivor of the purge. Rumor has it the Muddies
lost their secret-keeper too. They're scavengers,
copycats, thieves—the scourge of the dark sands.
For sport, we hunt them when the moon is full.

3. The Story of the Muddies

Tell us, Mother, should we journey to the north?
   we hear the Smaller Ones ask once again
and we the Bigger Ones become impatient.
   North? There is no such destination anymore—
no north, no south, no east, no west, only
   famine, drought, pestilence, and war. We might
as well ask, *Tell us, Mother, should we flee*
   the familiar and walk into the strange to suffer
among the unknown? We are doomed to die
   either way, but here we die among our kind,

not separated from the place that saw this
   collective born. We don't dare call it home—
home is a word as dead as mother, as sickening
   as the bowls the Muddies wear upon their heads.
We thought they looked as ridiculous as they
   were stupid until we saw a Muddy pee inside
of one. He mixed the sand into the liquid,
   and then used the gray clay to coat his skin.
When one dies the rest discard the stinky bowl
   into the fire pit—now a graveyard of skulls.

We used to pity them until our own skins
    began to blister and sore. We used to mock
their nakedness until our clothing grew heavy
    with our body's oils. We used to think we could
tame them, absorb them into our collective
    but they remained beyond repair. They had
joined us in the purge but never returned
    to their senses. They are the damaged cousins
who make us cringe because they remind us
    of the rage that entered us and never exited

them. They were banished to the other side
    of the crack in the earth, but they keep coming
back like loyal dogs. They mimic our rituals
    and cackle. They'll eat anything like hogs. When
they began to unsettle our sleep by invading
    our dreams we asked the poet for direction.
He was still breathing then though his eyes had
    sealed with slime. Maggots squirmed through
his stitched lips. He drew an arrow on the sand.
    We understand, we said, and readied for the chase.

4. In Pursuit

Mother disappeared. Or rather, the Smaller Ones
    fled and dragged her with them. They took
the last of the cats as well, breeding cages and all,
    and we the Bigger Ones will remember that
as our bellies grumble on the search. The crack
    in the earth is too wide for them, so they headed
west on their quest toward the north. We will
    find them eaten or dead. The collective now split
in half has become more vulnerable to an attack
    from the Muddies or the groups beyond the sands.

If you kill us you kill yourselves, the grown-ups said.
    And we killed them because we wanted those
parts of ourselves to be gone: that instinct for
    greed and gratification, the narcissism, the self-
indulgences, the self-centeredness of me, me, me.
    The I. I want, I need, I am, I take. So much I it was
easy to defeat a population that cheered its own
    annihilation, each person salivating at the spoils
the first victims of the purge left behind. By the time
    they banded together, there were fewer of them

than of us. We were a collective. We acted as one.

One goal, one purpose, one directive—to purge
Those Who Came Before, those who depleted what
few resources the world had left. When the crack
opened up like a wound on the earth, the oceans
receded, the animals died. It was time. The end
had arrived. *What goes around comes around,*
what goes around comes around, as the poet used to
say before we silenced his versification with thread.
We *are* what came around for *you,* knucklehead.

But the collective is only as strong as its size
and even if the Smaller Ones are hairless and
clumsy, they have working eyes and their limbs
will eventually grow strong enough to hold these
spears that protect us all. The us we had dreamed
falls apart in our hands and our worry turns to
rage. Foolish children. We the meek have reclaimed
this earth. Divided we fall. Maybe we'll forgive
them with kisses. Or maybe they'll deserve the wrath
coming for them once we find the right path.

5. Signs of the End of the World

The right path. The phrase echoes in our heads
　　as we travel west, away from the crack in the earth.
There is no way around it. Some say it connects
　　Tierra del Fuego to the North Pole and cuts deep
down to the core—a wound that lets the heat escape
　　each minute of the day. When all of the Américas
became a desert, dividing coast from coast, those
　　caught in the middle either sunk into the crevice
or sunk into despair. *The right path.* That's what
　　Those Who Came Before tried to sell us before hell

rose from the bowels of the planet to burn the air
　　in every lung. When the animals began to flee
and the birds headed east, we should have guessed
　　the doom had come upon us then. But the right path
was not to panic but to *study* these changes, *discuss*
　　policy, hold town meetings—negotiate. Catastrophe
was just another balloon to deflate. By the time
　　the ground beneath our feet began to shake, it
was already too late to save our cities, which had
　　turned to liquid we couldn't drink. Next came thirst.

What comedy to witness humans think they're
    in control of anything. The new collectives with
the old were just as tired and useless as the past.
    Their lifetime of mistake and misdirection was what
had killed us. Why repeat the leadership? Why
    allow the yesterday to roll its ancient wheels
into the present? Oh preachers of pretense, we
    silenced you. Oh teachers of nonsense, we erased
you. The future is ours, you all said, and the future
    arrived, bleak and black, but with much less room

to move around. A future without windows or doors,
    and one ugly hole in the ground that offers no escape.
What future is this? We asked. And Those Who Came
    Before simply shrugged their shoulders and shook
their heads. When the gas discharged from the opening
    we smelled the answer—sour odor of crimes against
the land and the centuries of death that had been buried
    there. Out flew centuries of damage and buried bodies
to hover above us like magpies shrieking: *The crack*
    in the earth, it is us. The crack in the earth, it is ours.

6. The Brittle Man of Clay

We come across a man who sits on the side of
     what used to be road, but which has been stopped
in its tracks by lava stone. From afar he looks
     like a Muddy. And as we approach we can see
his flesh is baked clay, but wrapped in cracks
     and chipped at the toes. He is even more ancient
than Mother, with sockets so swollen they swallow
     his eyes. *Should we pity this survivor or should we
break him down to shards?* we ask ourselves.
     We raise our fists over the pottery of his body

like hammers ready to strike, when he moves
     his mouth, releasing a groan that paralyzes us.
The sound strangely familiar—a hurt nudged
     awake in the recesses of our memory. We feel it
stir inside our brains and then it rains down
     to our hearts. It is not a groan. It is a song—
a spell so strong it is we who shatter like pots
     in a hurricane. We do not cry, we multiply.
All around us, more of us—the Smaller Ones
     inside us stumble out of broken Bigger Ones.

He sings to us of snow—feathers in the wind,
　　pure as light, the grace of innocence in how
it dared to embrace all, from the majesty
　　of buffalos to the tiny kindnesses of beetles.
No creature denied the kiss of gratitude for
　　bearing the burden of the snowflake's weight.
A sapling of a tree no less a part of the labor
　　than the muscular mountainside. *Community,*
equality, unity. He makes us long for gods that
　　our foolish ancestors once worshipped.

His song shrinks to a whisper and we have to
　　move in closer. We can't hear his words but
we can feel his breath, and that's when we
　　discover that our huddle is his purpose—
our bodies tightening around him like a forest.
　　He no longer naked and we a true collective
suddenly—one body with a dozen beating drums.
　　We squeeze the space out of the space between
our torsos and the brittle man of clay until he
　　scatters into freedom like a glorious dandelion.

7. Birth of the Trainees

The Muddies come upon us in our sleep—a
    deep sleep the clay man's final lullaby had put us
in, the first sleep we surrendered to, carefree
    and defenseless, our bare chests exposed like
a patch of butternut squash. When The Muddies
    break us open we spill into seeds. But we also
fight back—our spears sinking into the tar pits
    of their torsos, their blood slick as oil. How they
shriek like banshees when pierced. Our ears
    explode, erasing the memory of last night's song.

We must go on, we say, our collective sliced
    in half. Though this sacrifice is not without its
benefit—we conquered The Muddies, killing
    most of them and keeping those who lived
as slaves. We cannot call them slaves, however,
    or we risk repeating the stupidity of Those Who
Came Before, so we call them Trainees, as in,
    the souls we hope to save by training them
to be like us, to stink and wink and think like us.
    We begin by wiping off the mud. They'll burn

like us soon enough, pink and blistered, we
    will consume them into our collective and
replenish our loss. They are proficient diggers—
    their fingers razor-sharp—they tear into the soil
and uproot the vegetation fat with moisture
    that they sniff out with their keen mole noses.
We take away their finds. They whine at first,
    but when we share the goods with them they
surrender to the roles they have been given:
    to be the tools for those who gave them life.

At night, when they sneak out to the edge
    of the collective camp to mourn their dead, we
let them, knowing that by dawn they're ours
    again. We don't, however, allow them to replace
the pots they used to wear over their heads.
    We catch their pantomimes—covering their
skulls with their hands—we swat them off!
    The more persistent Trainees get their wrists
shackled to their ankles. Until they learn, we
    drag them on the trek by a rope around the neck.

8. Carnival of Cannibals

Headway: the shackled Trainee picks up a scent.
    Footprints on the sand and ash have been wiped
off by hot winds. We find a piece of cloth snagged
    on metal—the iron bone of useless artifact.
The Smaller Ones, in their childishness, might
    have found some joy in this graveyard of toys:
a train wreck, a fleet of planes plunged nose
    to the ground, a skeleton wheel with its knobby
joints collapsed in on itself, a boat designed
    to sail through clouds. But fantasy ends there.

In the caravan of cages, the insanity of misery:
    fur and hide cling to the bars like dried leaves,
hoof, fang and horn are lodged in the wood—proof
    of struggle—battle without victor because hunger
never exits once it makes a home. Human skulls.
    Spinal cord. We know this war. It's only a matter
of time before we too succumb to madness and
    begin to eat ourselves. *Let's go*, we whisper, our
movements slow as we sneak out of the carnival
    of cannibals intact, hoping the Smaller Ones did too.

The eyes of the famished predators are watching
　　from the tarps, waiting to pounce. They remain
still, unnerving us until the sound of grinding
　　bone and marrow fades with the horizon. Night
shelters us. The blisters on our skins release
　　their steam. We might have drifted into dream
just then but the Trainees crawled away to pray,
　　their senseless muttering a solace suddenly.
We resist the urge to enter their archaic haven
　　but our tongues, so dry, crave something in our

mouths. We let the shapes of sounds tumble
　　around and around—a whirlpool, a carousel,
that piece of cloth we found—how it flew off
　　its perch like a bird and then spun in the ground,
around and around, before we could catch it.
　　A sound so profound like laughter lifted our
spirits as we played with the cloth like a cat
　　with a mouse. Until it stopped moving. Its
redness a wound. We stood around it without
　　grieving it. We won't dare lament it now.

9. The Flying Men of Mexico

A quake awakes us. This time no one's crushed
    beneath a falling rock. The Trainees feed us
and we stroke them. They nuzzle the cups
    of our palms. They are strong as horses, but
as dumb, so we make their reigns with wire
    and line them up to haul the raft over the dunes.
The journey is long. We're getting too weak
    to speak, so we prod our horses left or right
with the sharp tip of a rod. Something streaks
    across the sky, startling our horses to a pause.

If birds still existed, we'd call the thing a hawk,
    but nothing with wings has flown since the end
of the world. Here it comes again: black angel,
    a dark moth so large it must have sputtered out
of the crack in the earth, a piece of carbon that
    took flight, took light, then came to life in the ruins.
Such sad paradise deserves this hellish bird to
    squawk and curse our desolation. We once heard
about the Flying Men of Mexico. Here they are,
    fiends that plunge to the earth like stars.

Another comes. Then another. A flock circling
   our hardscrabble collective. When they swoop
we crouch close to the ground to avoid their beaks
   and claws—machetes and sickle blades. Our
spears are useless on such evasive predators.
   The horses neigh in fear but weighed down
by the raft, they can't escape. They fall prey
   to the fury of Apocalipsixtlán. We scamper off
to hide beneath a shelter until the men ascend,
   their hunger sated. We will sleep with fear tonight.

An eerie calm descends over the land. We lick
   the salt off our skins but the taste of dread is bitter.
To spit is to waste hydration so we sit still inside
   the half shell of a church. Without the Trainees
we have no prayer, no lament, no holy sacrament.
   We sleep next to the broken cross, its Jesus limbs
attached but missing a torso. How far did such
   a creature drag its snail of a body before it got
snatched up by a Flying Man? Was there a second
   freedom in the drop before it smashed into rock?

10. Game of Whispers

On this first night without the Trainees we also
    recognize the twentieth moon. Another cycle
has spun past the era of the dead and we are
    still alive. We commemorate each period of
survival with a ceremonial game. We will miss
    the giggling of the Smaller Ones, who wait
impatiently for us the Bigger Ones to finish
    our exchange in the blackness. In the blackness,
animal noises—the lion assessing the lioness,
    the lion caressing the lion—a scratch, a screech,

and a roar—from exhaustion comes passion,
    from physical surrender reprieve. No famine, no
anguish. Mouth seeks water in a mouth—like
    a doe bending down at the lake to tongue its
shivering reflection. We whisper our names—
    syllable dissolving into syllable—a single spoon
stirring the pot. We lock our hands together, we
    drift away, acting out the roles of the Smaller Ones:
Our hearts hang from the rafters like bats. We
    like that. We are pleased. What else can we see?

Fireflies. Indeed. Where did they come from?
    The lights in our eyes. No. No lights allowed
inside. *But they're fireflies.* We don't disagree.
    But let's call them something else. *Lightning*
bugs! Tsk, tsk. Whisper, or they'll be frightened
    away. Now, think. Use that muscle or we risk
going numb, succumbing to thoughtlessness like
    The Ones Who Came Before. Now, imagine this:
Our teeth unpinned their stingers from our gums
    to dance like bees. *We can feel it!* Whisper, or

they'll drop like marbles on the floor and roll
    away. We don't want to lose a molar here.
We'll replace it with a rosary bead. We are not
    amused. We walked in complete and complete
we leave—collect all ears, which have paired
    into butterflies, chase after the litter of hands
and feet. We will have no children of God
    among us to hobble out like a seal, plump
and meaty meal for the vultures to pluck.
    The game of whispers is over? Yes, it is done.

11. Fate of the Smaller Ones

The absence of the Smaller Ones aches in the gut.

    We leave intact but we are incomplete. Sadness

protects us from the furious fireball—we scarcely

    feel its heat. Beneath us, a constant rumble—sand

shifting as it boils to madness. One more day without

    rain. We used to say it was heaven weeping, a cluster

of angels dropping tears down a pipe in the clouds.

    And then, just before the earth cracked open, heaven

bled. What vile massacre must have taken place

    everyday that week for the sky to drain only red.

We pick up a trail again: discarded cages, cloth

    that has been shredded in a brawl. Here and there,

locks of hair. Our smell is smeared in the evidence.

    We feel the pain in our heads, our backs, our legs,

reliving each violent strike and tug. Who ambushed

    them? The cannibals? The Flying Men? Another

hungry mob of hunters in coats of piss and mud?

    In our hearts we know that some of them survived

such an attack. The Smaller Ones are tough like that.

    We hear a faint mewing. We spring, devour the cat.

No doubt: the footprints of the Smaller Ones.

Relief replaces anger for the betrayal we once
felt. We follow the zigzag of a path—such child's
play. And then the texture of the ground begins
to change—from liquid sand to something coarse,
like salt. We taste it, but resist the urge to stuff
our mouths with the briny pleasure of this drug.

At the edges of the salt pond, a ring of skeletons
we haven't seen in ages—fish bones, antlered
skulls—a menagerie of casualties, all poisoned.

A lonely altar rests in the middle of this nest
of death. Mother sits, peaceful as a saint, watching
over her sleeping charges—the Smaller Ones,
scorched and spent, Mother's finger bones like
pacifiers strung around their necks. Oh innocents,
babies to the end. Little fighters, little soldiers, yes,
but impulsive. What tempting trap they wandered
into: a pool of candy for the taking. Mother let them
plunge and wade until their eyes began to froth.

They wilted into slugs to nap among the rot.

12. A Second Crack in the Earth

The pond of bones begins to rattle. Even Mother's
    throne collapses, her body disassembles. The ground
turns to quicksand as it trembles and swallows
    every socket, every thorn, every pebble. In a single
gulp the bed beneath the Smaller Ones swirls down
    a funnel. The earth has groaned like this before.
We know what to expect though it doesn't help
    us guess which plate will lift its crust and which
will crumble. The dust is blinding. It separates us
    as we scramble. Unknowingly, some of us run

right into the opening and plummet. We hear
    no screams. We hear no cough though we see us
spitting ink—the gas unleashed has cooked our
    lungs. Slowly the collective gathers in the shadow
of the clouds. We must guide our shattered spirits
    to a shelter before the mists release their acid.
In our ears the ringing doesn't stop. It will take
    a week and some of us will get the sickness—that
rabid urge to kill and tear apart what's whole.
    We fear no second crack. We fear another purge.

We wrap our arms around our bodies, swaying back
    and forth—we're motherless cradles, candle stubs
whose flames have melted down to callus. We are
    silent but for the piercing shrill inside our heads.
Cocooned in misery, we might have missed this
    spark of light entirely, but there it is, lifting heavy
chins from chests: a firefly—an actual firefly,
    beautiful bug from our fantasy game, a reality
here among the detritus of the world, rising from
    its dregs, a flicker, a flash, a wink of vital breath.

We try to catch the little star but it eludes our grasp.
    We let it be, it comes to rest upon a knee. Dare we
ask if this means the planet now spins in opposite
    direction? Does it begin to mend its ruptures, unclog
its river paths? The firefly fades but its ghost remains.
    No more dreams, no more questions. Sleep, tiny hope,
we do not know what threats or sorrows we'll
    encounter next. Tomorrow is a story for those who
make it through the present chronicle—uncertainty,
    scarcity—we the ephemeral have inherited this earth.

Acknowledgments

The Adroit Journal, American Poetry Review, Callaloo, Literary Hub, The Los Angeles Review, The Minnesota Review, The McNeese Review, Newton Literary, Orion, Poetry International.

"The Mexican Revolution," part 2 from "A Brief History of Fathers Searching for Their Sons" appears in *The Mighty Stream: Poems in Celebration of Martin Luther King,* Jackie Kay and Carolyn Forché, eds, Northumberland, UK: Bloodaxe Books, 2017.

Parts 1 and 2 from "A Brief History of Fathers Searching for Their Sons" were commissioned by the Smithsonian Asian Pacific American Center for an exhibit titled "CrossLines: A Culture Lab on Intersectionality."

Endless gratitude to the Rockefeller Foundation for a glorious one-month stay at the Rockefeller Center in Bellagio, Italy, where most of this book was drafted. And thank you, once again, to the USA Rolón Fellowship, which funded yet another month-long residency in Viejo San Juan, Puerto Rico, where this book was completed. The opening stanza of "Apocalipsixtlán: A Dystopian Long Poem" was inspired by Lebanese filmmaker Ali Cherri's *The Digger* (2015). "The Ghosts of Ludlow, 1914-2014" was inspired by Woody Guthrie's song "Ludlow Massacre" (1944). Many thanks to Danielle Holmes, who drove me to Ludlow, Colorado and who did much of the research that fueled the poem. Thank you to #TeamFourWayBooks for believing in my work. And much love to Dee Rees and Sarah M. Broom.

Rigoberto González is the author of seventeen books of poetry and prose, most recently the memoir *What Drowns the Flowers in Your Mouth*. His awards include Guggenheim, NEA, NYFA, and USA Rolón fellowships, the American Book Award from the Before Columbus Foundation, the Lenore Marshall Prize from the Academy of American Poets, and the Shelley Memorial Award from the Poetry Society of America. A critic-at-large for *The L.A. Times,* he sits on the board of trustees of the Association of Writers and Writing Programs (AWP) and is currently professor of English at Rutgers-Newark, the State University of New Jersey.

Publication of this book was made possible by grants and donations. We are also grateful to those individuals who participated in our 2018 Build a Book Program. They are:

Anonymous (11), Sally Ball, Vincent Bell, Jan Bender-Zanoni, Kristina Bicher, Laurel Blossom, Adam Bohanon, Betsy Bonner, Mary Brancaccio, Lee Briccetti, Jane Martha Brox, Carla & Steven Carlson, Caroline Carlson, Stephanie Chang, Tina Chang, Liza Charlesworth, Andrea Cohen, Machi Davis, Marjorie Deninger, Patrick Donnelly, Charles Douthat, Emily Flitter, Lukas Fauset, Monica Ferrell, Jennifer Franklin, Helen Fremont & Donna Thagard, Robert Fuentes & Martha Webster, Ryan George, Panio Gianopoulos, Chuck Gillett, Lauri Grossman, Julia Guez, Naomi Guttman & Jonathan Mead, Steven Haas, Lori Hauser, Mary & John Heilner, Ricardo Hernandez, Deming Holleran, Nathaniel Hutner, Janet Jackson, Rebecca Kaiser Gibson, David Lee, Jen Levitt, Howard Levy, Owen Lewis, Sara London & Dean Albarelli, David Long, Katie Longofono, Cynthia Lowen, Ralph & Mary Ann Lowen, Jacquelyn Malone, Fred Marchant, Donna Masini, Catherine McArthur, Nathan McClain, Richard McCormick, Victoria McCoy, Britt Melewski, Kamilah Moon, Beth Morris, Rebecca Okrent, Gregory Pardlo, Veronica Patterson, Jill Pearlman, Marcia & Chris Pelletiere, Maya Pindyck, Megan Pinto, Taylor Pitts, Eileen Pollack, Barbara Preminger, Kevin Prufer, Vinode Ramgopal, Martha Rhodes, Peter & Jill Schireson, Jason Schneiderman, Jane Scovel, Andrew Seligsohn & Martina Anderson, Soraya Shalforoosh, James Snyder & Krista Fragos, Ann St. Claire, Alice St. Claire-Long, Dorothy Tapper Goldman, Robin Taylor, Marjorie & Lew Tesser, Boris Thomas, Judith Thurman, Susan Walton, Calvin Wei, Bill Wenthe, Allison Benis White, Elizabeth Whittlesey, Rachel Wolff, Hao Wu, Anton Yakovlev, and Leah Zander.